# Me
# and
# Galileo.

Lyn Moir

ARROWHEAD
PRESS

*First published 2001 by:*
*Arrowhead Press*
*70 Clifton Road, Darlington,*
*Co. Durham, DL1 5DX*
*Tel: (01325) 260741*

*Typeset and printed by:*
*Arrowhead Press*

*Email: arrowhead.press@ntlworld.com*

ISBN 0-9540913-1-0

Cover colour printing and finishing by
Firpress Ltd. Workington  Cumbria

# CONTENTS

for Jack

## INTRODUCTION

I'd thought there would be bells
or fireworks, light, you know
the sort of thing, electric
current zigzagging the place.
I would have settled
for the comforting sensation
of a soft, creased leather glove.

You, just one hand shaken
amongst a dozen in the room,
were not what I expected.
No sparks, no noise;
only my skin: it liquefied
as in an acid bath and, bleached,
my bones reclothed themselves
in your warm flesh and were
no longer mine, while yours contrived
to infiltrate my hollow limbs,
left vacant by defection.

A fair exchange, a physical reaction,
or chemical, depending on your point
of view, something at any rate
which could not be reversed.

## ANTIMATTER MATTERS

Apart from the obvious
differences, of gender,
size and years, I'd thought that we
were mirror images,
opposing faces cut from
the same tree. We might have been
a Queen Anne bureau, twisting
burr veneer symmetrical,
glowing with the patina
of age. Or, face to face, we
might have graced an empty space
like chairs across a table.

Closer examination
proved our relationship was
inherently unstable –
two positives repel, as
do negatives: like and like
cannot tolerate the same
space, and mirror images
destroy each other. Banished
to non-existence by you,
my other self, dissolved in
darkness, I can watch you spark,
since everything is stardust
in the empire of the quark.

## A PHYSICAL RELATIONSHIP

He gazed into her eyes, pontificating
on superconductivity and such.
She smiled at him unheeding, mesmerised
by cadences of unfamiliar terms
and nodded, savouring the wine, thinking
of nothing so mundane as entropy, painting
a rosy future with a long-focus brush.

## CHASING RAINBOWS

It was you unravelled prisms
for me in your dry way, mocking
my ignorance, marvelling at how
I'd not been taught the principles
of natural phenomena.

You understood light, knew
its properties, its genesis,
its speed, its waves and how
it split itself into a spectral
glow projected onto sky or wall.

I knew nothing of the sun
except its rhythms, which spoke
not waves, whatever speed,
but danced erratically
in multicoloured words.

# GALILEO'S WINE

*Wine is light held together by water*
Galileo Galilei

It's late. Soft flickers on the wall
behind us fade as embers take
the place of fire. You throw a log
on, raise your glass as yellow blaze
comes up edged blue: seen through the wine
the flames are red and gold and red
again. I raise mine too and stare
at blood-stained light and then at you,
and huddle closer, licking first
your lips, the wine, then you again,
and alternating till the glow
dies down once more and we sit tight
while wind rattles the windows, snug
and sleepy, heated out and in
by passion's fire and liquid light.

# FIRST TANGO

Inept at dancing
and more so at romancing,
I longed for you to sweep me
to my feet, to keep me in your arms
around the floor. I saw you
linger at the door.
Then you walked past me,
cursed the stranger who harassed me,
the poor bugger was outclassed
by your cold arrogance
as we began to dance.
Who could ignore you, matador?

As the insistent beat
became the movement of our feet,
it sharpened senses, raising blood heat.
The change was bittersweet.
Behind the blank facade of your demeanour
there lurked a keener sense of the absurd:
so we gyrated, syncopated, sated,
stood out from the herd
in an arena of disapproving faces
went through our paces
as time and space grew blurred:
we tangoed, in a word.

Other couples started,
drew apart, and then departed.
We held the stage unchallenged,
proper dancers were outraged.
But we were fighters; holding me tighter
you hurled me to and fro, first fast, then slow.
I couldn't tell you how
I kept up with your antics
in that frantic, desperate rampage.
With you as Latin macho man
would I come up to scratch?
Oh man, we were a wow!

## A BREATH OF COLD AIR

We sat on broad, flat sandstone rocks
rimming the clear, sharp sea.
It was a fairly warm June day.

You swam while I sat dreamily
watching you eel for my delight,
wanton water turning your body blue.

I swam and you laughed endlessly;
I ottered and torpedoed, so
my casing shone in fine gunmetal too.

We huddled closely, laughing still,
goose-pimpled, pressed together,
salt water bound with sand as glue,

and faced the keen Siberian wind
knifing our flesh, a whaler
flensing blubber from his prey,

till we grew cold, as lovers do.

## OUT OF MY HANDS

I am in two minds about you,
myself and not-myself, the split
between my hemispheres complete
so that my right hand does not know
what tricks the left has up its sleeve.

I reach to touch you with my right.
The alien hand pulls it away:
it wants you for itself, to hold
or claw according to its whim,
taps sexy Latin rhythms while
its mate plays classical quintets,
both sets of fingertips vying
to print their rhythms on your skin.

As far as I know I have no
control over the sabotage
that one side of my brain inflicts
upon the other. This must make
my manner hard to predict. One
solution springs to mind: I must make
love to you, one hand held fast,
or even tied behind my back.

## ME AND GALILEO

It wasn't that I minded telescopes
as such, those cylinders of brass and glass
you stared through, finding intricate landscapes
in space; reversed, you turned their eye on me,
diminished thus to anonymity,
a pimple on the surface of your moon
or satellite in orbit round your sun.
You sucked me in, fed me your heresy
in golden, honeyed drops slipped from your tongue
to mine in secret. Holding me, you turned
me so I moved in time with you, each swing
like us, isochronous. But then, forewarned
by something in your manner, I declined
to climb the tower. I said I'd had enough.
You want to drop me? Do it on the ground:
I'm neither ball and chain nor bit of fluff.

## ONE DOWN

We used to do the Sunday crossword snug
and cosy after breakfast, warm from sleep
and coffee, spreading sheets of newsprint
on the floor. The fire once lit, we'd spend
the time untangling the anagrams
and other things. But then we split. I've done
Ximenes (Azed now) alone for years
and mostly get it out. And what of you?
How's your life now? I read the papers only
at weekends: retirement's like that, cut-backs.
For me to know, you'll have to organise
a Thursday death, or Friday just might do
if you've become the icon that you planned.

# THERMODYNAMICALLY YOURS

*Energy can be neither created nor destroyed,*
*it can only change from one form to another.*

A simple Newton's cradle, apple-strung,
my breasts hang waiting for your touch
to make them swing. My nipples raze
your chest, an extra set of fingertips
writing their signature on skin.
Your lower lip nuzzles my upper one,
nibbling, sucking, stroking while our tongues
meet gently, turning breath to appetite.

*Heat flows naturally from a hot object to a cold object; heat*
*will not flow spontaneously from a cold object to a hot object.*

Joined top and bottom in a seamless ring,
heat circling endlessly, a constant flow
of *chi* around the two in one, each half
becoming fire, returning heat to fill
the furnace of the partner's ravishing,
the glow continues when the bodies still.

*No device is possible whose sole effect is to transform*
*a given amount of heat completely into work.*

I think that's how it was, how strange
that I'd forget. It is too late too soon,
the pendulum draws near its sticking point.
Just touch my breasts again, or cup
one in your hand, unless your fingers too
have slowed. One  more exchange of heat
while movement's there? Time's running out,
or down, and even we grow cold.

## LUST

This unexpected sharer of my bed,
a presence I've not known for decades now,
forgotten for some time, let it be said,
although, years past, I'd welcome him, allow
his hands to wander at their will, yet how
can I surrender to his blandishments, or trust
his soft remembered touch, my lovely Lust?

His fingers light, his passion hard and rough
incites my eager, unaccustomed skin;
his breath, his tongue, his urgency – enough
to let once too familiar parts begin
to fuse, to make one body, yet no sin.
He enters me and all my senses must
combine with his before we come to dust.

## AMBUSHED

It's just as well the trend has turned away
from more old-fashioned scents. I could not bear
to have you stand before me every time
a fresh-faced, new-shaved man scattered his musk
in passing. As it is I find myself
sucking in breath, my stomach plummeting
as, swivelling to smile, I fail to catch
your shadow, brushing air with empty hand.

Your presence floats unbidden; then, as touch
takes over, cool sensation of your cheek,
shiny with waiting, then its sudden heat
warming its neighbour, so adjacent skin
becomes a single unit, and your body slips
from habit into mine, taking up space
in every organ. So much for passing time:
senses remember what the mind forgets.

## MOTHERING SUNDAY

There is no reason
for me to think of you today.
You are certainly not the father
of my children; I have no desire
to mother you nor to be treated
as your child. We have no family
relationship. I am daydreaming
in a Gertrude Stein-ish way,
because you are you *ad infinitum*
and that is what I am impelled to do:
which says far too much about me
and quite a lot about you.

## WINTER LOVE

Shall I still know you in your winter guise,
your thick hair white, your frame now brittle bones,
or shall I see you and not realise
this is my lover in his shrunken skin?
Some vague resemblance in your Baltic eyes
may strike a spark and laughter do the rest,
or blank incomprehension minimise
vibrations, mute the echoes of the past.
Or will your fingers, touching, recognise
my flesh in spite of mummifying time
which shrivels all? – though were that otherwise
there'd be no question: you'd still be the same
and so would I. Perhaps we have the chance,
should we still wish, to get it right for once.

## IMMUNE DEFICIENCY

They should have labelled it 'high risk'
at least, have plastered corridors with signs
denoting hazardous contaminants.
Would I have entered then? Of course. A moth
hell-bent on self-destruction would have flown
less carelessly.
             We talked, a ricochet
of random words, surreal syllables
simulating normal speech. Between us
we had aged seventy years, our body
cells had changed so many times that by no
reckoning could we have been the same,
outside or in. Communication seemed
light years away.
               Until a touch, when hands
grasped at each other, recognising friends
and lovers, flesh and skin apparently
unchanged, time flowing intravenously.
I'd seen no need to be inoculated:
I'd had this same disease before, suffered,
survived. Immune for life I was, I thought,
even as I recognised the tell-tale rise
in temperature, the shaking of the limbs,
the sudden drying of the throat.

They say a virus never dies, takes on
another form, lying in wait to catch
one unawares. I should have known
that hospitals are breeding places too.

## OL' BLUE EYES

There is a blue, just on the greenish
side of faded indigo, where when
I press my eyelids with my fingers,
sink in its warm inviting depths, I
freefall, whirling in the brilliant hue.

I had forgotten that the colour
of your eyes is just this shade. I stare
at them remembering the times they
mesmerised me, made me aware of
what my body wanted you to do.

Your hair has whitened, both our skins show
webs of deep lines edged over parchment
looser than it was. But your eyes glow
in the same bright blue that snared me when
I was young and green and loving you.

## NO EASY WAY

There is no easy way of silencing
your screaming skin. In unaccustomed folds
it cloaks protruding bones, tissue-thin
and sagged with loss of muscle tone.

An echo of that crooked, sexy smile
drifts past your face, storm cloud or sail
bellied before the wild October wind
which leaves, on passing, traces in the sand

outside your window. Seated there, behind
the insulating glass, you contemplate
the elements. I long to hold you, wait
and, motionless, unwittingly recall

the gentle warmth of your sure fingers. They
are turning into driftwood as I look,
or coral, spiky, bleached, ready to break
in needle splinters at a glance. The sea

has not yet chilled your eyes, although it laps
along the foreshore, creeping closer till
it meets them, then receding, but your lips
still shine, sleek pearl of empty mussel shells.

In gull-sharp shrieks your skin protests the touch
of whistling winds or lover's fingertips
alighting feather-soft upon your hands
but calms at the swift shadow of a kiss.

## GALILEO'S THERMOMETER

You dazzled me with erudite displays
of scientific hocus-pocus, globes
parading in their glory up and down
the tube as, powered by heat and cold, they rose
and fell sedately, glass balloons floating
in water simulating air.

I can remember you stroking my neck
as you enlightened me, delighting in
my childlike wonderment, touching my skin
as lightly as a puff of air, your tongue
lapping my earlobe like a rising tide,
in every way a sorcerer.

Catching the sun, the tube glows as they march,
its bubbles mesmerising with their calm
and preordained progression. It brings back
your prestidigitation and your spark,
as well as being a glass-blown condom with
a load of multicoloured balls.

## DON'T GET IT WRONG

Do not mistake the nature
of the warmth I seek in you:
not comfort from the chill air
of the night, but sudden heat
brought on by your embrace, your
tender hands, your urgent tongue.

Do not confuse my love for
you with mere affection: there
is that too, but this is lust,
stripped of its public face and
down to flesh and bone laid bare,
naked in its honesty.

## NOTHING

Even if we do nothing,
I want the length of you
pressed to me, cheek to toe
and skin to skin.

And while we do nothing,
lying quietly and breathing
mouth to mouth, I want
your hand along my thigh.

And if nothing turns to
something, well and good
and as it should be, but
if not, I need you still

as part of me.

## SPINECHILLING

The beading of your spine
runs long and straight. It always did,
but now each bump is more pronounced.
I trace my finger slowly
over peaks marking the decades
of a rosary of bone.

## MOUTH MUSIC

When I spoke with you again I found
an echo of my native language,
long neglected, lining every word,
and took from you vocabulary,
pebbles unaccustomed in my mouth
fitting underneath my tongue like teeth
ground smooth by years of uneasy dreams.

## POINT OF VIEW

To you I may appear
a rainbow, bright and steady,
arched against cloud, but
in my eyes I am only
the component drops,
colourless, falling
and scurrying, blown
by the slightest wind.

## WEIGHTY MATTERS

I picture you staring out
over a slightly different sea –
towards the Isle of May, perhaps,
or an unsuspecting trawler –
pondering the frequency of clouds,
the gravity of chuckie-stanes
or, wanting to stretch your legs a bit,
the tensile strength of water.

## GOLDEN OLDIES

We lost our inhibitions when
we danced home in the dark,
arms around each other,
from a night out at the Old.
I fancied our relationship
would never be the same
after you as Marlon Brando
sang with me as what's-her-name,
surprising the old biddies
at their curtain-twitching games
while we, more drunk on air than rum,
sashayed half the length of North Street
to the rhythm of that bell.

And, husky-voiced after another flick
– shown this time at the New –
I breathed another classic song,
my lips brushing your ear, and you
murmured to me of Paris
as the sea came crashing in,
but the sands were really desert
and our time wasn't yet
when you were Bogart and I Bergman,
cheek to cheek as time went by.

On other nights you cooked
exotic meals. We dined alone
and afterwards sat sipping by the fire
an unassuming claret, gazing
interspersed with kissing. Wide-eyed waif,
I loved your languid, sexy look
when I was Audrey Hepburn
romanced by cool Greg Peck
and time stood still.

They show them all as classics now,
nostalgia on the box
resurrecting old emotions
in the flicker of an eye.
We're too old for this caper,
though I like to think that you
might at times remember us
as Burton-Taylor, Grant-Loren
or any pairing from those named above,
as stars unchanged on screen
keep their allure, which is obscene
as, vari-focalled, we increase
the volume for the reruns of our love.

## THE PHOTOGRAPH

Those were your glory days. The sun allowed
sharp shadows on your face to underline
the strong cast of your features, painting fine
leaf shapes over your cheek, making the proud
line of your bearing subtler than the loud
'*Just look at me!*' I had expected. '*Mine.*'
my body cried, short-circuiting my brain.
My mentors warned me then: '*He thinks he's God.*'

But cotton-head, betrayed by hormones, sex
stronger than reason, headier than drugs,
went her unheeding way, and damn the cost,
oblivious of censure. Who protects
the lunatics of love, trapped by the tug
of raw emotion, who rescues the lost?

That, though, was *then*, and *now* has undermined
our self-perceptions, leaving us as mere
projections of our former selves, obscure
perversions of attractive forms, designed
computer-aging, features twisted, lined
parchments in palimpsest, criss-crossed with years,
our bones distorted, senses gone, cocksure
displays of arrogance left well behind.

And yet... I find your withered flesh affects
me greatly, as its younger form once did;
your skin, your hands, your twisted smile, your eyes,
have me as mesmerised as ever. Sex
can always trick us, even when our heads
object. You too? Who'd have it otherwise?

## DEFAULT MODE

I seem to be programmed for loving you,
just as a new-hatched duckling, casting round
with new-born black bead eye, fastens on
the nearest moving creature: imprinted
for life. My settings have been configured
on a 'read only' basis, so nothing you
nor I may do can change the circuitry.

No built-in obsolescence here: the software
runs smoothly as before; one might suspect
upgrading on the sly, since hardware is
long past its date. My life is in a loop
that anti-virus programmes can't sort out,
and when I try removing the root cause,
my love for you, I cannot uninstall.

## ONCE MORE, WITH FEELING...

It shouldn't be,
The whole of me
bemused, entranced by you...
Time was we sang,
alarm bells rang
each time I danced with you...
Sparks blew the sky
apart when I
flirted, romanced with you...

That's how the love song should have gone
to chronicle that magic time
when you and I were young and one...
you are the crazy reason I'm
not scared to let love in once more,
although emotions cut and thrust
with all the force they did before...
I ran the gamut then,
why do I feel I must
suffer it all again?
Who is there left to trust?
Just me and you:
it's *déjà vu*...

all over again.

## NO MOURNING, BY REQUEST

I'm sorry you witnessed such an ill-mannered display: no sense
of timing, grief, one never knows how it will strike, or when.
You said no tears, no regrets, no sadness – easy for you
on the receiving end. And I'm not sad at all, for you;
for me, I'm desolate. How can the empty space
you leave behind not suck me in, transport me to
a deeper, darker place? Or can our symmetry support
another, parallel existence, where time means nothing
and you, bright sun, erase all shadows from the past.

## ROUND THE HOUSES

*Tongues of Clatto, Nether Magask, Morton of Blebo...*

Delighting in names we drive to escape from the gossips, the spite
of inquisitive neighbours, mere speculators, spying and clyping

*...Pitscottie, Kininmonth, Baldinnie, Drumcarro, Ladeddie, Denork,
Upper Magus, Nether Strathkinness, Rummond, Cauldside, Strathtyrum*

and home to a welcoming fire. Or, spreading our wings, thumbing
our noses at all interference, we drive out brazenly, finding

*Over Rankeillour, Fernie, Lindifferon, Cunnoquhie, Cantyhall,
Monimail, Melville, Grange of Lindores, Lumquhat, Wester Rossie*

and many's the glass we raise to our finds. Now, driving to see you,
caught in a time-lock, clutching at signposts to link then to now

*Wester Balrymonth, Lambieletham, Gilmerton, Lathockar, Lingo,
Lathones, Lathallan, Balcarres, Balmakin, Pitcorthie, Kilconquhar*

to Elie, Earlsferry and you in your eyrie overlooking the Forth.
I need many more farm names to ground me, returning alone by the coast

*Ardross, Craigiewells, Coal Farm, Crawhill, Rennyhill, Cornceres,
Kirkmay, Sypsies, Wormiston, Grassmiston, Cambo, Boghall...*

towards the kirk spires, the martyred cathedral, the ramparts of learning

*...Pitmilly, Pitmullen, Kingask, Kinkell, Brownhills, Balmungo*

back to the harbour, the links, the wind and the waves, on my own.

## SAD SONG

Sing no sad songs for you? I wouldn't try,
I wouldn't raise my voice to sing with you
still in the room, as you would be, one way
or another. You'd laugh and so would I,
just as we used to, each protesting at
the other's sound – old corncrake voice, you'd keep
the tune but scrape, while I had tone in spades,
yet could not stay in key. Unlikely pair
of lovebirds, that's for sure, we seemed to share
so little; yet together we would make
passable sound. That's how it was, at least
as I remember it – who'd be the first
to crack a smile, to catch the other's eye,
to grin, to laugh, to hold each other close:
no contest, ever, always a dead heat,
a pair of idiots reduced to tears,
as I am now. Me sing? No bloody fear.

Some of these poems first appeared in the following magazines:

*Brass Butterfly, Equinox, Fife Fringe, The Frogmore Papers, The Interpreter's House, Making Worlds (Headland Books)*, *Poetry Scotland, The Red Wheelbarrow, Seam, South.*

*Sad Song* won first prize in the Split the Lark Open Competition 2001.